Daily Peace

31 Days of Peace in Practice

an
i see peace
companion
pocket reader

...a little peace in your pocket...

by maya gonzalez

For Zai, Sky, & Matthew

Copyright © 2015 by Maya Christina Gonzalez.
Published by Reflection Press, San Francisco, California.
All rights reserved. Printed in the USA
ISBN 978-0-9843799-5-8
Library of Congress Control Number: 2015956959
Book Design by Matthew SG

"create a new reality" ~ www.reflectionpress.com
Reflection Press is an independent publisher of radical children's books
and works that expand spiritual and cultural awareness.

This book is a companion reader to *I See Peace* book & journal
 • More info at: www.reflectionpress.com/iseepeace

Believing is Seeing Online Course.
This book also grew out of Maya's online course, *Believing is Seeing:
Daily Journal of Transformation* taught through School of the Free Mind.
The 31 day course uses the *I See Peace* book as a framework and guide
coupled with this *Daily Peace* pocket reader and the *Believing is Seeing*
workbook to transform everyday habits and open up to peace.
 • More about the course: www.schoolofthefreemind.com/peace

peace love trust now peace

Introduction

This little book is the perfect pocket size to take everywhere you go. Perfect when paired with the *i see peace* book & journal as it follows and expands on each spread of the book. Perfect on its own to continue the practice of peace.

create a new reality

unCommon fruit series

reflection press

"I am Peace. Peace is my teacher.
I am my greatest teacher."

peace belongs to
EVERYONE!

Through gentle, repetitive behaviors you become more aware of your thoughts and consequently your beliefs about your self, your world, what's possible, and more. You begin by playing with your beliefs about peace as a way to not only bring more peace into your life and the world, but also to learn how to transform beliefs that are not serving you.

This work has the potential to be as deep and transformative as you wish it to be. I encourage you to go slow and steady. You have the potential to learn great things about yourself, about the world we live in and how we can create lasting and far reaching change. I already have immense faith in you. I know the power that lies within you. Take a moment to pause and sense that power, all that potential already expressed and all that lies latent within your deepest self.

What you do here matters.

You change the world as you change yourself.

Peace begins now. With every
breath I breathe in peace, with
every breath I breathe out stress.
For a moment I allow the entire
last year to rest on my breath--
as I breathe in, I hold onto each
moment of love deep in my being
and as I breathe out, I let go of
each worry, fear, hurt and anger
and I breathe in again.
Peace begins now.

DAY 1

❋ Daily Thought

With the momentum of new beginnings and the power that rises from within, we begin. We will be working with our beliefs as we open ourselves up to see a new life, a new way of being, even create a new, more powerful habit of support for ourselves and the planet.

Take a moment and review the last year. What aches and pains, what joys and triumphs, what lessons learned or unlearned? Notice everything. When you acknowledge and accept what is without judgment, you open doors to greater creative flow.

This is the day to begin.

Peace begins now.

✳ Affirmation _____ for DAY 2

When I bring awareness to my thoughts and beliefs they begin to transform. I begin to open up to the real power of my thoughts and beliefs. And even though I feel like I still have a lot to learn, I trust that this will make my learning more effective until it is effortless.

DAY 2
❀ Daily Thought

Peace. What is peace?
The question inside of this question is, do I feel peace? We cannot fully know something if we haven't had the experience ourselves. It is always best to begin where you are. Honestly look at your life, your heart, your private self and ask,
do I feel peace?
You may be confused about whether you feel peace or not. It may seem that you feel peace in certain areas or certain times and not others.
Determine if peace touches all of your life or if it is isolated to certain areas.
If you find that you feel peace, pay close attention to what this feeling is.
How would you explain it to someone.
If you feel like you don't really know what peace is personally and you don't think you feel peace in general, this is equally good to notice. **Bringing awareness immediately begins changing things.**

❋ Affirmation ___ for DAY 3

I can see through any limited thinking as I open up to the possibility that deep and constant peace is available to me at all times. My natural state of being is peaceful, keeping me strong and flexible through all the amazing times in my life. My thinking is opening up now.

DAY 3

Often we have *"pie in the sky"* notions of what peace is.

Lofty, brightly lit illusions that give a sense of hope and possibility, but are not actually felt, experienced and relatable on a more mundane level. Seeing through the illusion of what we would like to think peace is begins to bring real peace more into reach.

Open up to see if you have illusions about peace. Illusions that may have kept peace unattainable.

✳ Affirmation — for DAY 4

Peace is every moment. For this
moment I let go of my thoughts
of worry and responsibility and I
simply listen to myself say, peace
is every moment. I don't have
to believe it. I can just listen to
myself say it. This is my moment.
This is my peace.
Peace is every moment.

DAY 4

✳ Daily Thought

Using peace as our learning ground to see through illusions, we can begin to see through other illusions we may have. Our experience in society often leads us to create rules or requirements for living, for example *"once this happens, then I can feel peace."* Because of its physical, external focus, the Western world of thought is built on what is provable, linear and rational. What falls outside of these parameters, things like intuition, creativity and imagination are often repressed, denied or judged... this automatically creates a low threshold of possibility for something as core to our being as peace. We've been convinced that we're being good or responsible if we are worrying or striving first and that if we're good enough long enough, we may experience peace at some later point. Being weighed down with guilt, obligation or regret replaces the possibility of inner peace in every moment.

❋ Affirmation — for DAY 5

Today I feel peace in my feet.
Whether my feet touch the ground
or not, my feet are connected to
the Earth and I feel peace. I am a
natural part of all things and here I
belong. I feel peace in my feet.

DAY 5

✽ Daily Thought

Again, what is peace?

After sifting through illusion and other limitations to your experience, you may have a better understanding of peace and just how close or far it is for you. You may recognize that inner peace is not dependent on anything outside of you. It is a sense that rises from the core of your being. It already belongs to you. It is a timeless, unshakable feeling of rightness that radiates out. Consult your heart of hearts, have you ever felt inner peace? Again, acknowledging that you haven't had this feeling, begins to change things.

**Sometimes my experiences do
not need words.** They grow in
my heart and give me a feeling of
peace that is mine deep and true.
A peace that cannot be touched.
It exists. It endures.
It is my eternal core.

DAY 6

✳ Daily Thought

Whether we know peace or not, it can be hard to put into words. The dictionary says that peace is freedom from disturbance, quiet, tranquility, harmony and calm. These are external representations of peace. Inner peace is defined as *"a state of being mentally and spiritually at peace, with enough knowledge and understanding to keep oneself strong in the face of discord or stress. Being 'at peace' is considered by many to be healthy and the opposite of being stressed or anxious."* The trick is that we can get the idea that our inner or personal peace is supposed to be the same as the concept of outer peace. But if peace is every moment, peace can encompass all feelings. Your peace may be loud and rambunctious at times. Peace comes in every flavor possible. Only you know what your peace feels like and only your words or images can fully express that peace. Play with the idea of expanding your concept of what peace means.

**My deep internal, eternal peace
touches everything in my life.**
Although I cannot always feel it, I
can trust that I am surrounded by
peace. Peace is in me.

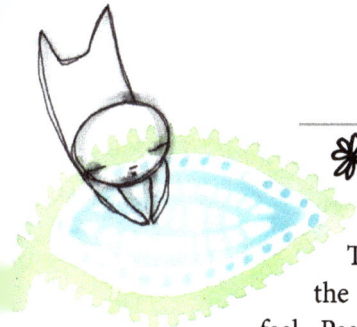

The more you feel peace, the more peace you can feel. Peace spreads out, grows roots, reaches up. Because peace is a natural aspect of your core self, as you become more aware of peace, you will not be able to find an end to it, because there is no end to you. You may find places where your beliefs do not yet permit you to go, but in all things, in all places, there is peace. The more facile you are at seeing and transforming the limitations in your thinking and your beliefs, the more peace is available to you. Those false boundaries will be seen for what they are, old thinking waiting to become new. As you learn to transform your thoughts and beliefs, you will become truly free.

✳ Affirmation ___ for DAY 8

I am deserving of peace because I am peace. In every way throughout my day I attract peace. But no matter what is going on in my life, there is a constant sense of connection with my deep inner core where I am peace.
I am peace.

DAY 8

Many of us have been taught in our families, our communities or through society, knee jerk beliefs in good and bad, right and wrong, punishment and reward. We may even convince ourselves that we do not deserve peace or peace is not available because of this kind of thinking. We may think we've done something wrong and it may be true. For whatever reasons, we may have behaved in less than our most idealistic way at times. We may have shame. We may even have hurt others. Or we may have been in the position of being hurt. Others may have used power over us. We may feel damaged. Or used. In one way or another, we may question our value and doubt our worth on a very deep fundamental level. But now please know, peace comes from your core, it is untouched by your beliefs and experiences. Peace is a constant and eternal part of your inner self. No matter what. No matter what. Your core is peace.

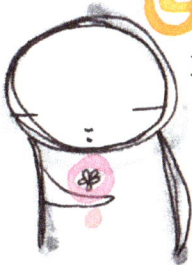

**It is easy for peace to grow in
my life because I am peace.**
Creating more and more peace is
perfectly natural for me.
I am like a tree of peace, a sea of
peace, a sky of peace.

DAY 9

❋ Daily Thought

Unlike happiness, peace is
unconditional.

Peace is not dependent on
anything on the outside, because peace
comes from the inside. Once you become familiar
with your inner landscape and are more and
more able to see your beliefs, you will be able to
see through the beliefs that do not fully support
your deepest self. As you see through the beliefs
that do not support you, you will naturally begin
to open up to new beliefs that do support you.
Most of our beliefs develop unconsciously. Now
you can begin to create
the beliefs you want--
consciously.

It is wise to listen to my heart and my hunches. I am learning to listen to my inner self. This connects me to the peace at my core and supports greater creative flow within and between all areas of my life.

DAY 10
✤ Daily Thought

Becoming familiar with your inner terrain means paying attention to your thoughts, feelings and intuitions.

Many of us barely notice what we're thinking or feeling we're so focused on what we need to do in the physical world. Paying attention to our inner selves can feel foolish and indulgent. Many of us are also so well indoctrinated into caretaking others that it can feel wrong to attend to yourself first. With this in mind, getting to know your inner self is like any relationship. It takes time to develop. You need to listen and try to understand. Be kind and curious. This builds trust and allows you to go deeper through experience. We have become so disconnected from our inner selves, we must allow a relationship to develop slowly and surely. Almost like a good friend, listen to your thoughts. Listen to what's underneath the thoughts in your head.

Listen to your heart and your hunches. This will create more flow in your life.

✳ Affirmation ___ for DAY 11

Without judgment
I see all of me,
I listen to all of me,
I accept all of me.

DAY 11

Daily Thought

Like any good friend, listen to yourself with an open mind. Try to understand yourself with a kind heart and remember the challenges and lessons of your life. We often pick up unsupportive beliefs unconsciously, during stressful or traumatic experiences and when we're very young. These are not truths. Only beliefs we picked up to get by. When our beliefs are not visible, they can feel like truths and we can easily judge ourselves as good or bad, right or wrong. There is no need for judgment, only awareness and patience. Opening up to see your beliefs for what they are, changes EVERYTHING. This is how you create lasting change, by working with your beliefs first and foremost.

I belong here in perfect order,
I am a natural, creative being
of the world.

DAY 12

❀ Daily Thought

There is a natural way that each of us is designed to be. A unique, creative expression of our full self living our full life. The more in line our beliefs come with our inner self, the greater our peace and the more we live this natural way. This lets you access your immense creative flow while supporting everything and everyone else on their path to becoming their full selves.

✳ Affirmation for DAY 13

In peace I stand, in peace I am, wholly myself and open to others. As I commit more and more to knowing my inner self and allowing my full truth to flow through my being and my life, I naturally draw people and relationships that support me into my life.

DAY 13

When we stand in peace, we will notice others in our life and in the world that also stand in peace. Since we are all peace at our core, we can begin to feel the similarities between all of us and sense our underlying oneness. This allows us to open up to more good feelings not only within ourselves but through our connection with others. Our core peace begins within. When we let it move out, when we are whole and solid in ourselves, when we see peace, we serve as a blueprint and a magnet that naturally draws us into relationship with people who support our truest, deepest self.

❋ Affirmation for DAY 14

I open to the ever unfolding fullness of my own peace and I desire this for everything and everyone. Peace in the earth, peace in the sea, peace in the skies and peace in me. Peace for the creatures, and peace for the trees and everything that grows and flows and shows itself.
I am peace and so peace I see.

DAY 14

❋ Daily Thought

When we begin to see how unique and valuable our own inner peace is, what a big difference it makes in our own lives, we can then understand more and more how true this must be for everyone on the planet. We are all one yet each of us, individually, is a valuable and necessary expression. We need everyone's unique peace. Once we grasp the perfect uniqueness of our own peace, we can also appreciate that everyone's peace is different and simply want others to feel their own inner peace, however that manifests.

✳ Affirmation for DAY 15

I sense the deep inner peace within every person on earth and our connection. I open up to new thoughts and ways of being in relationship that supports the deep inner peace within each of us.
I see peace in me.
I see peace in my life.
I see peace in my country.
I see peace in the world.

DAY 15

Very few have experienced a full inner peace on earth at this time. It is new territory and we can only imagine from our very inexperienced perspective, what kind of thoughts become possible when we are truly surrounded by a world of people at peace. *What would be important and necessary in the world? What would fall away? What kind of relationships? What kind of society?* We will begin to understand these possibilities more and more because as we have greater peace, we will be drawn to situations and people of greater peace. And together we will begin thinking those thoughts that were not available to us before. And together we will create something new that was not possible before.

Inner peace is my guide in relationships. As I change and commit to my inner peace, I trust that peace has my back because peace is my core. With this deep inner part of myself, I create relationships that support my whole, true self.

DAY 16

As we begin to appreciate and understand on deeper and more personal levels how important and how unique everyone's peace is, we come to see that there are infinite paths to peace. There is no one right path, no one right way. And this is reflected in our relationships. Relationships adjust and evolve as we do, especially as we commit to peace and listening to our inner self. It can be disconcerting if we've built our life on outside expectations. People want us to be who we were to them, even if we weren't being true to ourselves. Committing to peace may initially bring adjustment to relationships. Sometimes this adjustment means that we must let go of the old form in order for a new, more supportive form to rise. Trust that as you allow your relationships to transform through peace, you are supported. Peace has your back, as someone put it. Often relationships serve their purpose, last their time and come to completion. Letting go in peace and honoring what you've learned is a powerful step toward peace.

✽ Affirmation for DAY 17

I commit to my own inner
peace.
My peace is independent of
anyone else's peace.

There are many things to learn and many paths to peace. Respecting our path and the path of others is very important. We are not supposed to force our connections, we are already *one*. At times it is only by disengaging and separating that peace can grow. The most effective thing we can do is to commit to our own peace and know that only each person can commit to their own peace. The more you understand your deep inner core of peace, the faster and more assured your knowing will be about what relationships and connections are right for you. As you create more peaceful relationships, there is more peace and more to learn about creating peace.

I commit to my peace and I respect that others must commit to theirs. I let go of nonproductive conflict. I let go of thinking I know what's right for others as I let go of thinking anyone outside of me knows what is ultimately right for me. I embrace peace in all its many forms.
I do not judge peace.

DAY 18

We are beginning to see how important it is to be our true self. This puts us into direct contact with peace. This is true for everyone. And only our self can do it. No one can do it for us and we can't do it for anyone else. We learn to let other people be themselves on their path as much as we need that from other people. Live and let live essentially. Or, heal and let heal. A valuable thing to understand is that peace does not mean fluffy love all the time. Sometimes peace means different degrees of separation and that's ok. There is a peace in that. So often we think we have to engage and work it all out, when the truth is we may be in very different places. Sometimes there is growth in conflict, but often we are engaged in conflict more for conflict's sake than to resolve anything. Recognizing what is productive engagement and letting go of nonproductive engagement is ok. It's ok to not have relationships with everyone. Live and let live in PEACE. With our family, at work, with our friends, in community, at school, everywhere.

❋ Affirmation for DAY 19

No matter what is passing through me and my life, the essence of my deepest self is peace. Peace is the fierce flower of my creative soul. I have only to turn my attention to my deep self to access this peace. Because I can sense this truth, I am open to knowing and clarifying the beliefs I have that stand in the way of this. I trust that peace is mine. I will find my way.

DAY 19

No matter what is passing through you or your life, the essence of your deepest self is peace. It's no surprise that this right here is the essence of deep inner peace. No matter what happens you can have this foundation of knowing. Peace is the essence of your deep inner self and the essence of all things, that creative force that flows through everything. You can have that broad, cosmic perspective that everything is ok. Really. No matter what happens. No matter what feelings pass through you. No matter the loss, the change, the grittiness of the moment. There is a fierce flower that is your soul. It is eternal and this is really who you are. This is the greatest lesson to be learned from being yourself fully from the inside out. As this becomes more of how you identify yourself then the whole nature of your life changes.
You will still learn things, but you can know that you are more and so much less than you thought you were.

✻ Affirmation __for DAY 20__

I ask my inner self to guide my daily self toward peace. This is my life and I consciously create the life I desire.
I desire peace because I am peace.

DAY 20

We have been taught
to look away, to look
outside of ourselves
at the physical world
for literally everything,
even our sense of self, even our own inner peace.
Because we have been looking away, peace can
feel fleeting. Sometimes easy to see, sometimes
we're trying so hard and we just can't see a thing.

But peace is there.

Slow down. Trust. Listen.

Remember, peace is the natural state of the
inner self. *The more you develop a relationship
with your inner self, the easier it is to access your
peace.* Creating a connection between your inner
self and your daily self, or as I like to think of
it, the self that drives the car and uses the stove,
brings greater peace into your everyday living.
Remember *to listen to yourself*, that self under
the self, those beliefs under the thoughts, and the
feelings that don't move through but stay.

I live in a safe universe. I open
my mind and my heart to the true
essence within myself and within
all that I see. There is peace, there
is cooperation, there is belonging
in all directions. The more I shift
my perspective in this way, the
more I will understand.
I live in a safe universe.

DAY 21

When we look at the state of the world it can seem foolhardy to believe in peace. Everywhere we look the world is being framed and reported as dog-eat-dog. But we've been falsely taught that the world is survival of the fittest. Current research exposes that it is only through grand cooperation that we and all beings, survive. Cooperation is the true nature of nature. It was stressed out humans, separated from their inner self, their core peace, who judged nature as dangerous. We can be part of this new understanding of the world by shifting our perspective on ourselves and nature as a whole. We are not inherently competitive. We are in fact inherently cooperative. Just as we are, at our core, peace. I don't think we can underestimate the effects of this shift in perspective from a competitive survival stance to a cooperative peaceful stance. We are not what we thought and neither is the world.

❀ Affirmation for DAY 22

I entertain the possibility that I can feel peace all the time. I respect that it is a journey but that just by committing to this direction I create movement. I trust that peace is my core and that the more I connect with my inner self, the more I know peace. Again, I entertain the possibility that I can feel peace all the time.

As we begin to
see our beliefs
and their effect
on our inner self,
our body and

DAY 22

✳ Daily Thought

our life, we can begin to entertain the possibility of consciously choosing beliefs for ourselves. We can stop looking outside and start looking inside to our inner self and our core peace for what beliefs we want to hold. Seeing a belief for what it is, feeling the emotions that keep it in place and learning to listen to the inner self are important steps and may, in and of themselves, transform a belief. Often however, there is a leap of faith moment, that moment when we have to put down our old way of thinking and entertain the possibility of a whole new way. While many of us think that we desire peace all the time, in the day to day experience, we may find that we have "limits" on how much peace we are willing to experience. For many of us that leap of faith is simply about believing that we are meant to feel free and peaceful all the time. We are accustomed to living in such a small part of ourselves, at first it may feel like a stretch to become more of who we are. It may even feel uncomfortable. But that is just the old way passing away. Committing to yourself and your living in this way is worth it. Every step counts on the journey to the inner self and you can trust that peace awaits at your homecoming.

❋ Affirmation ___ for DAY 23

I believe. I believe. I believe...
as I change my beliefs,
I change not only myself,
I change the world.
I believe.

DAY 23

✳ Daily Thought

There is peace everywhere. We're living amidst a wild array of peacefulness, a virtual forest of luxuriant peace, freewheeling and prolific. Inside and out.

It takes a lot to blind us to the true, creative power everywhere to be seen and felt. But our entire way of thinking in the Western world has created and locked a state of blindness into place. That's why we go to the most powerful source of creation to transform our lives, we work with our beliefs. By changing our beliefs, we are not courting denial or ignorance about the state of the world. We are bravely opening up to see what is really real, beyond mainstream media, beyond limiting beliefs picked up as a small child, beyond societal expectations, beyond the materially focused, Western thought. With the knowledge that our core is peace, we can change our beliefs. We can change the world.

❋ Affirmation ___ for DAY 24

In the sky I see peace.
On the earth I see peace.
Peace is everywhere nature and
I am the heart of nature.
I am peace. With every step, with
every breath I feel my belonging.
I am here. I am here. I am here.

DAY 24

There are two places where we can come into direct contact with the truth of the inner self. One lies within, as you have been exploring. The other great within, is nature. And truly, nature is all around us. Dirt, birds, sky, wind, weather. Even in urban environments, nature is everywhere. Paying attention to nature is a powerful way to understand the nature of the inner self. The deep, constant need for growth, flow, cooperation, expansion. Nature also shows us the grittiness, the eternal, even the melancholy along with exuberance, wild and free. It is the face of peace.

When we look within, we are facing nature because we are a part of nature. We are looking deep into the heart of nature by looking deep into our own heart. When we look out at nature, we are also meeting our self because we are a part of nature. Looking out at nature is just as much a way of looking deep into our own heart.

✳ Affirmation for DAY 25

I value my inner self and know that my core is peace. Everything is possible, as I transform my beliefs, I transform my life. These simple truths I hold dear and do not forget. I allow this wisdom to grow in me, increase with each day, become the breath I breathe.

DAY 25

❋ Daily Thought

The more you practice, the more you play; the more you open yourself up to seek, the more you will find! You will come into greater contact with and awareness of your inner self, and your peace will naturally increase. As you get to know yourself more in this way, you will find that the journey is yours. I see peace will become your words because they belong to all of us. Or they will transform into new words. You will teach us your wisdom of peace in the way only you can. We need you here with us. We need your peace. As you need ours. Your peace is my peace. My peace is yours. Changing your beliefs to value your inner self and recognize the peace that is at your core can become your way of life. Everything within and without you can change from this place. I believe.

**Every day, I open myself more
to the truth of my inner self,
the depth of my peace and
my amazing power to create.**
My self, my body, my life are the
artful expression of my inner self.
Trusting that peace is my core, I
create a safe universe inside and
out. I am free to create the life I
imagine.
I am free to be safe and powerful.

You are becoming more and more familiar with your inner self and your deep inner core of peace. You're beginning to see and your thinking is shifting. You are becoming more you as you come into contact with your true self. This is the most powerful and supported position for absolutely everything in your life. It is an especially powerful position for manifesting what you want.

Pay attention to how you've brought peace into your life. Feel how you have opened up to peace and how it feels when you are in the flow. Peace has been teaching you all along how to create other things in your life. Within you lies the power to create anything. This is the source of your true power. It is not out there in the world. It is right here within you. If you want to affect your outer world in a real, substantial way that lasts, you must begin within. You must begin with you.

✳ Affirmation for DAY 27

I am a limitless, creative being of infinite peace. I trust that my inner self and my daily self are aligned to assist in the perfect creation of the life I desire. The more I let go into these truths, the more effortless and graceful my life unfolds.

DAY 27

❋ Daily Thought

There is no limit to what you can create in your life. Through peace you will begin to learn that anything is possible. There is an infinity, an eternity within you. Allow the wisdom of your peace to continue to teach you about how to create everything. Peace is the essence of your deep inner core and this part of you desires more and deeper peace, more you, your deep essence aligning with your daily self, creating your life like the art that it is. You can trust and relax into this part of yourself. This is home. Here. Now. You may not be who you thought you were. The world may not even be what you thought it was. But ironically, you may find that you are exactly who you always thought you were, deep down inside. And the world is as magic now as it was in some childhood moment when you could still see.

✳ Affirmation for DAY 28

I am my greatest teacher.
I teach myself in every
moment. All I have to do is
pay attention to my inner self.
I am peace.
Peace is my teacher.
I am my greatest teacher.

DAY 28

You are your greatest teacher. Establishing a foundation of trust with your inner self provides you with the most important tool you can have. You can trust that. You can trust you and your belonging and your perfection. All you ever need to do is wake up to who you truly are. You will greet peace all around you, as your inner world becomes reflected in your outer world. You are safe. What you create from this place can only make you stronger. It will multiply your sense of peace and creative power because that is your true essence. You fulfill a natural cycle of being.

The more I sense my individual
creative style, the more
effortless creating becomes.
Peace and creativity are my
natural states.

DAY 29

❊ Daily Thought

Through these initial steps of creating peace, you can sense how your own unique creative force moves through you. You can sense what your most authentic and intuitive way of creating art AND peace feels like? This is the same with everything you want to create. Sensing the feel of your individual creative style helps you to access and enhance your creative power as you learn to ride your natural ebb and flow.

Some creations take time with numerous layers of underpainting. Some creations are spontaneous like the swift touch of ink on paper. You will have both. Keep your eyes open to all the different ways you create in your life. Trust that like creating art on a blank page, you have created peace in places where before there seemed to be none. These experiences put you in touch with your creative power. This prepares you to consciously create bigger and bigger things in all areas of your life.

❋ Affirmation for DAY 30

I am in this body and heart to
be my full self. It is in being
my full self that I fulfill my
purpose here and bring the
greatest amount of peace that I
can to earth.

DAY 30

Sometimes it is only in hindsight that we can fully receive and appreciate the journey we have been on, the courage we have had, the leaps we have made, the real peace we have created. You are not the same person who began this book. You will never be the same. You are more now and because of that, you will become even MORE, naturally. More creative, more peace filled. The door has been opened.

Now you know,
you create your own reality-the more you are you, the better you create—EVERYTHING!
It is worth the journey. It is why you're here.
It is why we need you.

More and more of my life
expresses my full self and
my deep peace.

✿ Daily Thought

Making peace as much of a habit as your morning routine is just the beginning. When we approach all of life this way, when the inner self and peace are the foundation of life, everything becomes rooted in the very heart of who we are in the biggest, deepest sense. Our body, our relationships, our work, our family, our community and more…Your life becomes one great flow between the inside and the outside, the living and the being become one. This makes you strong as a person and more and more of us strong as a people.

You are changing the world.

This is the new wave of revolution.

This revolution begins within and cannot fail because it is who you are.

Believing is seeing.

I see peace in you.

❋ About the Author

Maya Gonzalez has been teaching about the power of creativity to heal and transform for over 20 years. An acclaimed fine artist, award-winning children's book author and artist, progressive educator and activist, and radical peacemaker, she lives and plays in San Francisco with her partner and kids.

www.mayagonzalez.com

Other Titles in the unCommon Fruit Series:

i see peace
book/journal

i see peace **e-book**

yo veo la paz
book/journal

Believing is Seeing:
daily journal of transformation
(31 Day Workbook)

www.ingramcontent.com/pod-product-compliance
Lightning Source LLC
Chambersburg PA
CBHW071103040426
42443CB00013B/3380